Profitable Forex.

The ultimate guide for trader.

Your Gift

I wanted to show my appreciation that you support my work so I've put together a free gift for you.

http://bonusfreebook.org/

Just visit the link above to download it now.

I know you will love this gift.

If you like this book, you can see and buy my other books on this link:

Thank you for attention!

With love,

Adam Clark

Contents

INTRODUCTION

In the finance industry, exchange rate is defined as the rate at which a currency can be or will be exchanged for another currency. It can also be described as the value of a currency in comparison with another currency. For instance, the interbank exchange rate of United States dollar to a Japanese Yen is ¥114 or equivalent to 1$. That interbank exchange rate means that every $1 is the same as ¥114. In this case, if you have $1 and go to a bank asking for Japanese Yen you will be given ¥114. This rate is fixed and determined by the foreign exchange markets. In this financial market, there are many buyers and sellers who do continuous trading of various currencies every second of every minute. This trading is carried out for 24 hours every day apart from weekends and public holidays. Exchange rates are different for every country. The main aim of exchange rates is due to be used when traveling. When people move from one country to another they need to change money from their currency to the currency of the country they are going to. For instance, when you leave the United States and going to Europe, it is mandatory that you change the United States dollar ($) into the European Euro. This is because you can not use the dollar in Europe. With time, traders had to invent new ways of making money from these fluctuating exchange rates. The exchange rates keep changing every minute. They keep rising and falling and this gives traders an opportunity to buy when at the rate lowers and sell when it goes up. This requires traders to be vigilant at all times throughout the day. However, this is not the only way traders make money from the exchange rates. There are many other ways of making money from Forex exchange and this book is going to dig deep into all the possible options. Trading in foreign exchange rates nowadays has gotten easier due to the various advancements in technology that has allowed the traders to trade online instead of physically visiting Forex exchange financial institutions. The online trading is accomplished by opening various trading accounts with brokers who manage the trading on your behalf but the profits get credited to your online account which you can later transfer to your bank account and withdraw. This guide is going to explore all the dynamics of Forex exchange and the ways a trader can make money from this fluctuation of exchange rates. Before getting into the main action, there are a couple of terms that you need to fully understand so as to be conversant with the business. These terms are the types of exchange rates that you will encounter during trading. These terms are:

➢ **Reverse rate:** when doing an exchange in currencies, there is a buy-and-sell price. The buy price is the price at which the financial institution will buy the currency from you. The sell price is the price which the financial institution is going to use when selling the currency to you. For example, if you have a dollar and you want to buy Kenyan shilling, the buy price at the bank would be 1$= Ksh110, and the sell price would be Ksh110.50= 1$. This means that you can sell 100$ at 110*100= Ksh11000. You may then decide to change back the Kenyan Shillings into dollars again so as to make a profit. In this case, you will wait for the rates to go down until you are able to change back the Kenyan shillings into dollars and attain more dollars than the initial investment. This is basically what the reverse rate is all about. It is a method that brings out a bit lower returns but when dealing with large sums of money you can make great profit margins.

➢ **Cross rate**: this can be described as the comparison of exchange rates between the two currencies without involving the dollar in any way. Practically, this is the exchange rates of currency A and currency C gotten from the actual rates of exchange between currency A and currency B. For example, you can find the exchange rate between the Japanese Yen and the British Pound in relation to the Swiss Franc. This will be done by finding the value of the Swiss Franc in relation to the Pound and then comparing the value of the Swiss Franc to the Japanese Yen. In this case, you will assess the value of the Japanese Yen against the

British pound but by using the value of both currencies against the Swiss Franc.

> **Spot rate**: a spot rate is also called the spot price. This is the value of a currency at the current time or the moment of doing the quote in question. The spot rate is constantly changing every minute for exchange rates. The spot rates might rise or even fall sometimes depending on market forces in the world economy. This change is mostly influenced by the demand. This is the willingness of the buyers to buy the currency and the sellers' willingness to sell the currency. The amount that sellers are willing to accept from the buyers determines the spot rates of various currencies in the Forex exchange markets. The spot rate is also influenced by the current market value in relation to the expected or future market value of the currency. The future values are derived from the use of various forecasting methods applied by the traders. The forecasts allow the traders to know the value of the currency in the future by using the past information and current situations in the market. This greatly assists the traders in making buying and selling decisions. The spot rate in some instances can also be referred to as the straightforward rate, outright rate or even the benchmark rate. It is important to also note that spot rates do not only exist in Forex exchange

markets but also in all other markets dealing with assets both long term and short term.

Chapter 1.
The fundamental analysis

The basic macroeconomic indicators:

You would wonder what are the macroeconomic indicators? These are the indicators that are used by various financial analysts to make forecasts on future prices and behavior of various financial assets, in this case being Forex. The behavior of these indicators dictates either a rise or fall in the price of financial assets. This macroeconomic indicator helps in the preparation of macroeconomic data that is useful in the provision of the forecasts and decision-making by the traders.

GDP (gross domestic product)

This vital figure well describes the growth of a country and the expected future economic situation. The measurement of this figure is done quarterly but the results are published annually. Gross Domestic Product therefore can be adequately described as the total sum of all the goods and services that have been produced by a country over a one-year period. When the GDP calculated is positive, the country is said to be in a good economic state. However, when the GDP is either 0 or negative, the economic status of the country is weak. In terms of Forex, when the GDP is positive and the economy is stable, the currency of a country is usually very strong and highly-priced in the world's Forex market. This is a dangerous time to buy since the currency is not likely to go higher; instead the likeability of the value of the currency going down is rising. On the other hand, when the GDP is either 0 or negative and the economic status of a country is weak, the currency value goes down. It becomes a weak currency in the global Forex market. This is a great time to buy since the currency value is low and there is more likeability of the value of the currency rising when the economy starts to improve. That is basically how the GDP is used in the decision-making process in the traders. It is a very useful indicator of the economy of a country and speculation on the likely fluctuations in the currency prices on a global basis.

Industrial production

The federal government issues a monthly report on industrial production. The industrial production report contains all the data on the manufacturing of utilities in the given country. This report greatly helps the traders in studying the structure of the economy. This is because the country's manufacturing industry greatly determines the economic structure of that country. Industrial production together with the other ratios aid in the calculation of capacity utilization ratios in every industry. The analysis using these ratios is done by selecting a benchmark year and then comparing it with the current year and, thus, basing on the realized behavior, the traders can make a suitable forecast. Industrial production is a useful ratio since the behavior of the manufacturing industries in a country indicates the possibilities of the onset or the offset of inflation. Inflation has adverse effects on the currency of a country.

PPI (price production index)

This group of indices measures the level of change in selling prices received by producers domestically from the sellers over the given time. This differs from the cost price index that measures the change in prices as received from the perspective of the buyer. P.P.I is mostly used at the production level. As discussed earlier, the prices of commodities and production levels determine the state of the economy. P.P.I can be used to forecast by the use of the information from the past years.

Current account balance

This is one of the two components of balances of payments of a country. The other one is the capital account balance. Current account balance is a trade balance that consists of all net cash transfers in a country, trade balances (the differences between the total exports and total imports of a country) and net factor income (difference between total payments done to people domestically from foreign investments and total payments made to people abroad from investments they have made domestically). The current account balance index basically shows the level of a country's competitiveness against the others on a global basis. When a country's current account balance is positive, it is referred to as a net lender to the other countries it is trading with globally. When the current account balance is negative it is referred to as a net borrower from the other countries it trades with. Together with the GDP, the current account balance can be used to measure a country's economical strength and consequently, the strength of the currency. The indices can also be used to forecast the future value of a currency from the future expected status of the economy.

Trade balance

This is also known as the balance of trade. As explained earlier it is the difference between a country's exports and imports to determine whether the country is a lender or a borrower. For example, if Argentina has total exports equaling 750 billion dollars, and its import value is 1trillion dollars, the country is said to be having a negative trade balance or a trade deficit. This means the country is a borrower since the difference is negative. Vice versa, if Argentina has 1 trillion in exports value, and 750 billion in imports value, it is said to be having a trade surplus. This means the country is a lender; it doesn't borrow to import. This mostly correlates with the political stability and economic status of a country. Trade balance sometimes also represents the level of foreign investment brought to the country.

Unemployment rate.

This is the rate of people qualified to work but still seeking jobs. The unemployment data is an important index since it gives the information about the current state of the economy. When the economy is weak, the unemployment rate is very high. When the economy is stable the unemployment rate is low. When the unemployment rate is constant then the economy is stable. The unemployment data gives a review of the state of the economy in a country. This is why traders can easily use this data to know the current state of the economy and consequently the behavior of the currency value in the Forex market.

Chapter 2

The Technical Analysis

Provisions.

Technical analysis is the use of past data to determine the outcomes in the future. Forex traders use both technical and fundamental analysis to predict the future behavior of currency values. Technical analysis works on various provisions and principles. These being:

- ➢ All the market prices are a reflection of information relevant and impacting the market. This is what makes the technical indicators be the valid tools of forecasting and studying of the prices of the particular currencies. Indicators are derived from the data collected from a given economy.
- ➢ It is believed by analysts that trends tend to repeat over the time since the behavior of the traders also keeps changing all the time. This is what makes the historical information such a good tool to be used during the technical and fundamental analysis. Analysts study the past information on the trends of prices in order to make the future predictions for the Forex items.

The graphical method

One of the three assumptions is that the trends from the past tend to end up repeating themselves time and again. In that case, in order to see the larger-scale picture, the analysts draw the charts with the data from the past and study how the trends are going. Traders study and identify the patterns to a point they can be able to draw a conclusion on the future or a certain currency. The main chart patterns known are continuation and reversal. A reversal chart is that where the prior pattern repeats itself once completed. A continuation chart is that one where the prior pattern continues once completed.

Reversal patterns

A good example of reversal charts is the head and shoulders. On completion of the prior trend, the pattern reverses itself. The chart is characterized by the three peaks. However, the middle tip is the highest peak. The middle peak is, therefore, called the head since it is the highest. The other two are relatively lower than the middle one. They are mostly equal and consequently termed as the shoulders. The neckline represents the two lows between the three peaks. In these lows, the traders are told to be keen for a reversal of the pattern or a breakdown of support level.

- *Continuation*

A good example of continuation chart is the cup and handle. In this type of chart used by the bulls mostly, the upward trend pauses but continues once the pattern has been confirmed.

- *Triangle*

Triangles are among the most used charts by many traders. Their main advantage over the others is the frequency of their occurrence. Ascending, symmetrical and descending triangles are the most common examples of triangle charts. Symmetrical triangles occur when the two trend lines meet at the middle insinuating the possibility of a breakout. Ascending triangles possess a flat upper and rising lower trend line that insinuates the possibility of an upward breakout. Descending triangles are the opposite of the ascending triangles. They have flat lower trend line.

The Mathematical Analysis **Moving's**

Moving is the average gauges' momentum as well as confirming the patterns. They also define the support and resistance areas. Moving averages do the smoothening out of the noise. Noise can be described as the fluctuations in the prices and volumes. Moving averages are the lagging indicators and, therefore, their reaction is mostly a result of things that have already happened. This makes it more of an explanative indicator instead of a predictive indicator. It helps in understanding the things that have already happened in a given market. Different types of moving averages basically rely on a similar premise. The difference between them is the number of variables available. These types include exponential moving average, simple moving average and weighted moving average.

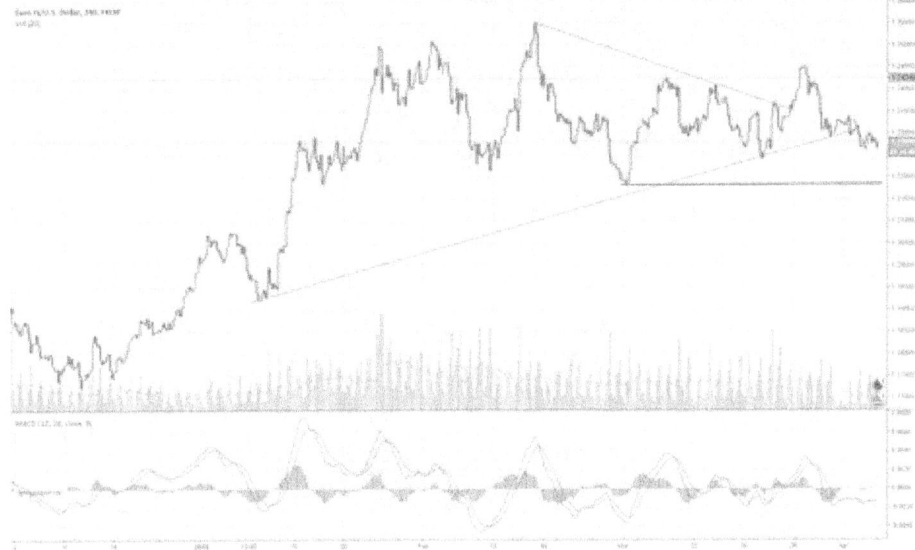

- *Stochastic*

The stochastic oscillator does a comparison between the closing price of securities and the prior price fluctuations that have been happening over a specific period of time. The sensitivity of this mathematical analysis can be reduced by adjusting the timelines. This analysis is used to determine the overbought and oversold securities in the market.

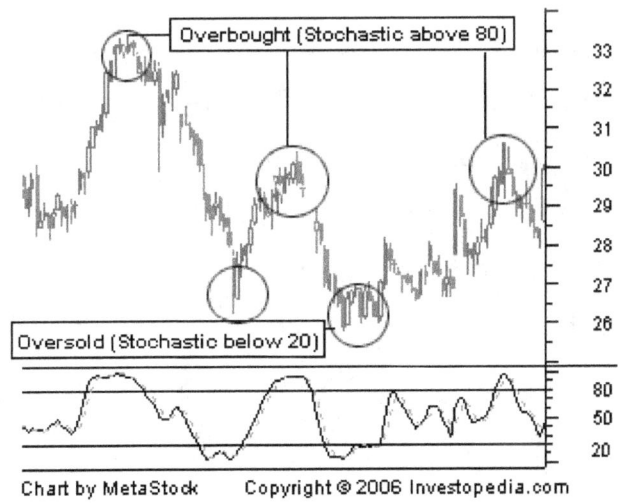

Chart by MetaStock   Copyright © 2006 Investopedia.com

- *MACD*

Moving average convergence divergence (MACD) is a momentum indicator that follows the trend and shows how two moving averages of prices are related. They are interpreted as crossovers, divergence, and dramatic rise.

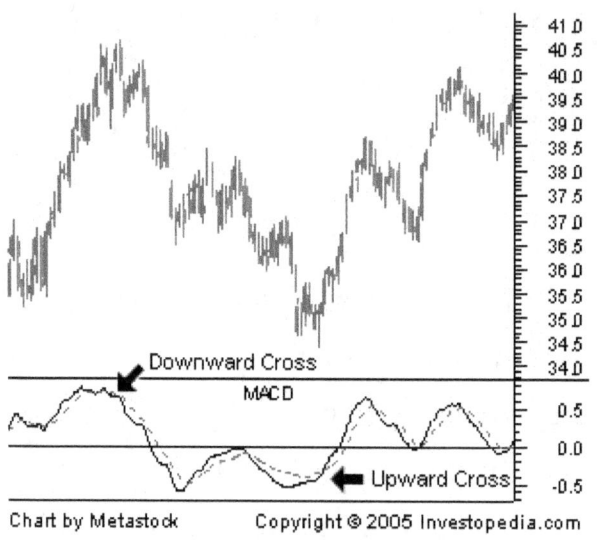

DMI

The directional movement indicator signals the traders on the strength and the direction of a trend. This is very useful for the determination of possible future outcomes. DMI was invented in 1978 by J. Wielder and greatly helps the traders in either taking a long or short position. This is because this indicator shows when the trends are likely to be strong and when they are weak. In short, DIM assists in maximizing the profits.

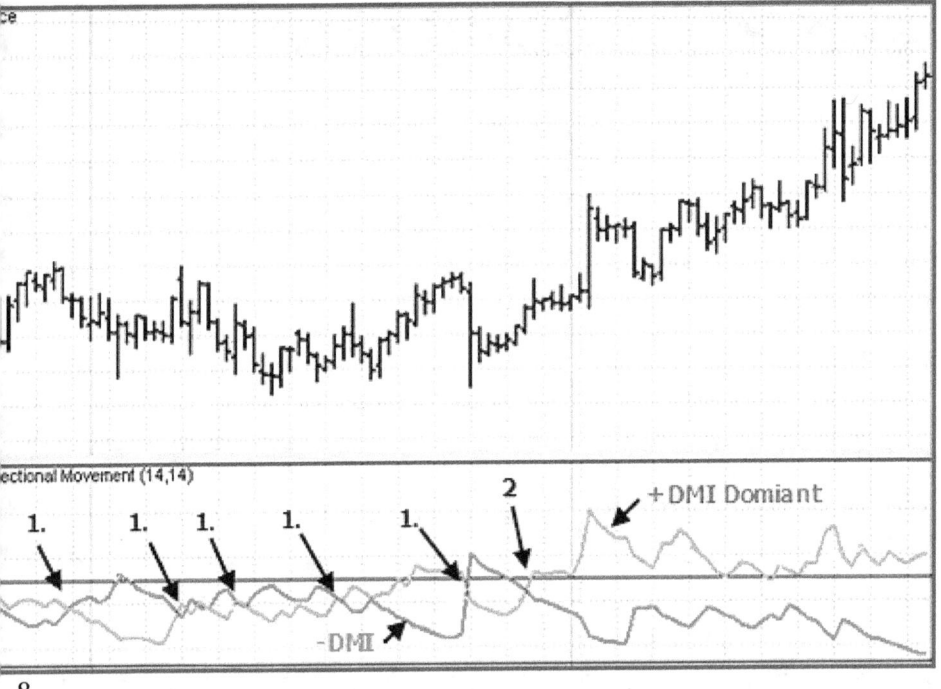

8

- *Divergence*

Price momentum is key when determining the strengths of a trend. Fast momentum means the trend is strong while the slow momentum means a weak trend that is most likely to change soon. Divergence can be described as the difference between the indicator and the price. Divergence shows an uptrend and downtrend. The uptrend is when the price is higher than the indicator and the downtrend is when the price is lower than the indicator. Divergence indices assist a trader in knowing the behavior of the price and, therefore, making an informed decision.

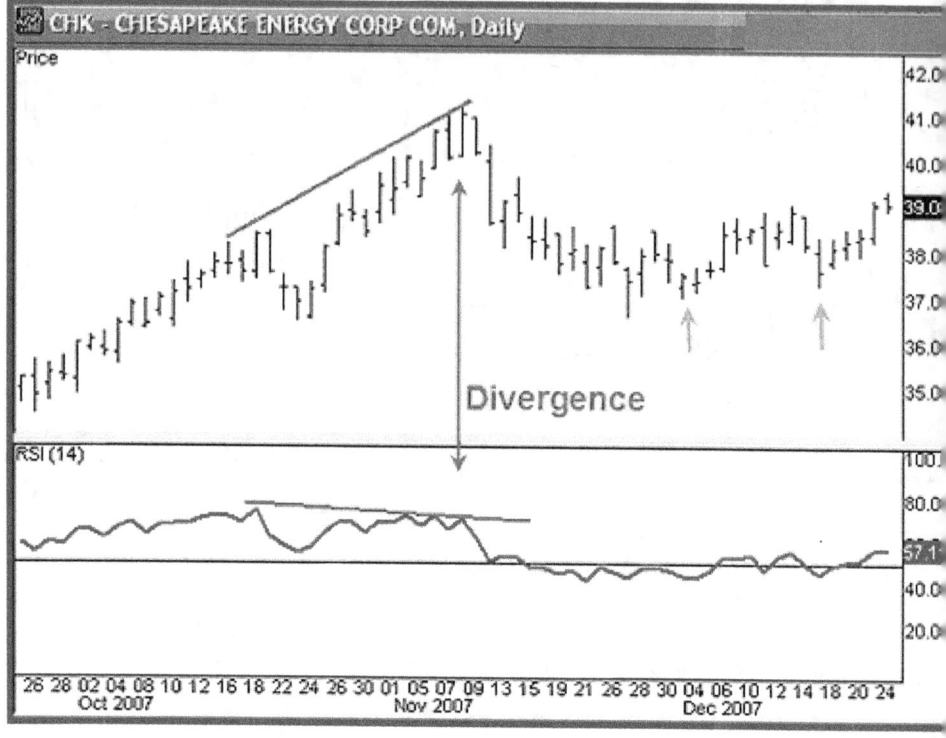

- *William's percent range (%R)*

This indicator is comparable to the stochastic oscillator in that it measures the overbought and oversold securities. It establishes the points of entry and exit in the market. It is calculated as:

%R = (Highest High – Closing Price) / (Highest High – Lowest Low) x -100

it compares the closing prices presently and the highs and lows of the security.

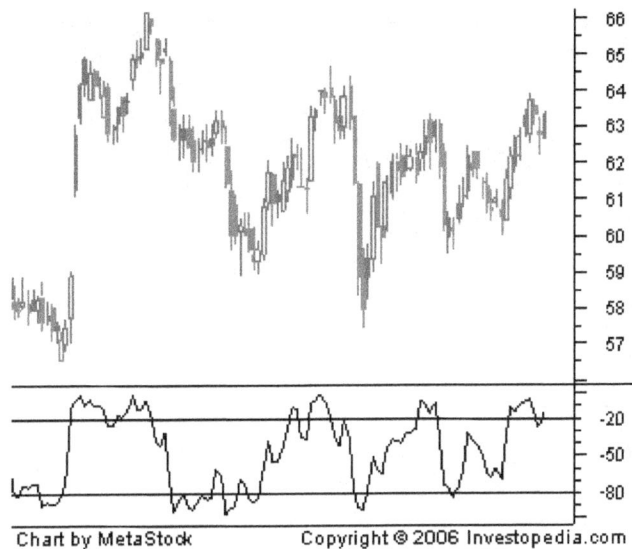

Chapter 3

Elliot wave theory

Main provisions.

Ralph Nelson Elliot developed this theory in the 1920's. The main principle of his theory was that securities' behavior in the market is somehow chaotic and keeps going in cycles repetitively. The prices are expected to follow certain cyclic patterns that are repetitive and, therefore, predictable.

    1. *Examples of waves*

        a.   *Impulse wave.*

The behavior is broken down into 5 subsections or rather five sub-waves. These sub-waves are labeled 1 to 5. They develop the inside part of the trend channel. Sometimes the movements can, however, go outside the channels.

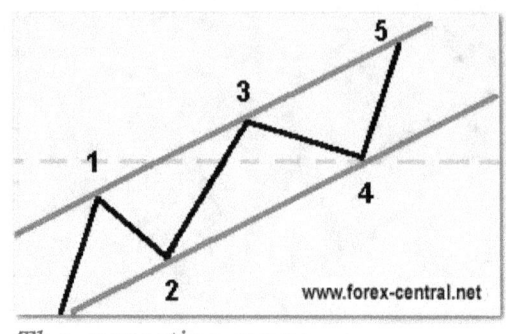

b.

c.   *The corrective wave.*

They fall into four sub-categories:

- Flat correction
- The triangle
- The zig-zag
- Double 3 and triple 3.

         i.   *The zig-zag.*

This wave features the 5 descending and the 3 descending waves.

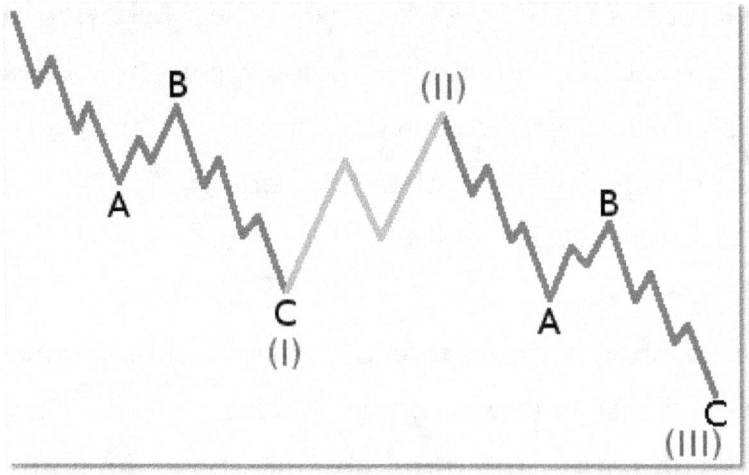

         ii.   *Flat correction.*

The start of wave A is almost at per with the submitting of wave B.

Wave C and A are right across each other.

This pattern is 3-3-5 and basically, it breaks down the flat correction.

The Flat correction is broken down further into 2 subgroups: irregular flat correction and doubly irregular flat correction.

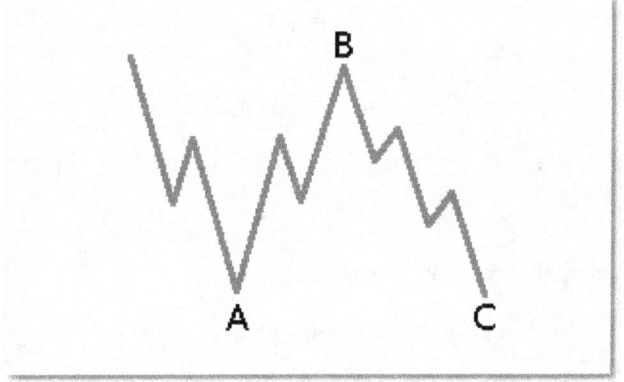

iii.   The triangle.

They are divided into four different types:

- Ascending
- Open
- Closed
- Descending.

Waves in a triangular design have 5 sub-waves denoted as a, b, c, d, e.

These sub waves are made in 3 waves and a trendline is present.

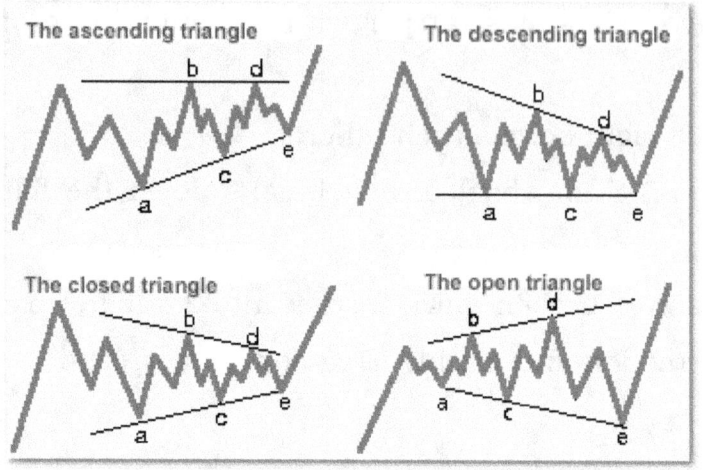

iv.   Double 3 and triple 3.

They are broken down into 7 sub waves that are comprised of:

- Corrective waves with 3 sub-waves.
- Second corrective wave with three sub-waves
- Transaction wave with one sub-wave.

A triple three differs from a double 3 in that instead of the two corrective waves only, there is also a third corrective wave with three sub-waves.

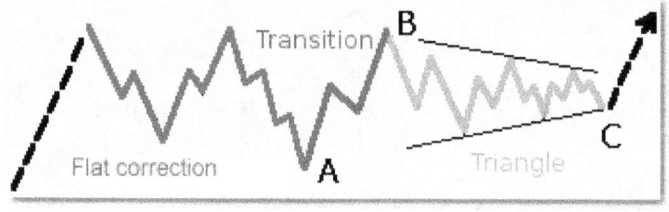

Fibonacci numbers – the basis of wave theory

The mathematical foundation of the Elliot wave theory is the Finobucci numbers. In technical analysis, they measure the corrective ways. They are usually adapted to various indicators. Waves are measured by ratios (Finobucci numbers). Finobucci series possesses various characteristics. The series is basically started by 1 and adding the previous number to attain the next number. For example, 0+1=1, 1+1=2, 2+1=3, 3+2=5, 5+3=8, 8+5=13, 13+8=21, 21+13=34, 34+21=55, 55+34=89,

The properties of the series are numerous and interesting:

- The ratio of any particular number to the next is 0.618/61.8% (as seen in 34/55 = 0.618)
- The ratio of any particular number to any other found two places to its right is 0.382. (as seen in 34/89 = 0.382).
- The ratio of any particular number to any other found three places apart or its right is 0.236 (as seen in 21/89 = 0.236).

These ratio relationships are data that is used to determine the price behaviors in a trend.

Chapter 4

Money management & tactics of trading.

If you provide two different traders with the same probability resources, still their earnings will be different. This is a result of money management tactics applied by the traders. Poor money management frequently causes traders to go into losses. In case of any losses, traders need to make certain amounts of profits in order to recover. The table below shows the losses made in percentage and the percentage profits needed to recover.

Amount of equity lost	Amount of return necessary to restore to original equity value.
25%	33%
50%	100%
75%	400%
90%	1000%

The big one.

The information in the above table is well-known to all the traders. However, most traders keep ignoring this information waiting for the big one. The big one is a term used to refer to the big break. Most traders might go on losses year after year without looking deeper into their money management just expecting that one big deal that will turn them into millionaires and help them retire early. Most traders begin their career with the vision of the big one and this makes them end up making massive losses to an extent of being unable to bounce back from their profits. At the same time, it is true that it is possible for some people like, George Soros, to make huge profits reaching billions in a day by shortening the pound.

Learning through lessons.

Traders, however, have a chance of controlling this loss. They can control the risk by stop the losses. Larry Hite, a famous trader, admits he followed the advice that one should not risk over 1% of their total equity. Many traders lack the discipline of following this principle and end up learning the hard way through incurring huge losses and struggling to recover. With the advice, a trader can fail 30 times and still end up having 70% of their net equity intact. This is because they follow the rule of not risking more than 1% of their total equity.

Money management styles.

Practically speaking, there are two main ways of money management. A trader can choose to take frequent small stops and eye the few big wins that come their way, or they can reduce the frequency of stops and increase the small wins. These two strategies are equally effective in the end. The choice of the strategy is mostly due to the personality of a trader. The first one needs a risk-taker who can handle psychological pain since the losses may be many with a few large wins. The second needs less risk-taking enthuse. There are various types of stops as explained below:

- Equity stop: this is usually the simplest of all stops. The trader only uses a predetermined amount of investment for the account. Mostly the common metric is 2% of the account. However, some more aggressive speculators may choose to take 5% as their equity stop. This is, however, very risky since 10 losses may turn into 50% of total losses. The main disadvantage of equity stops is that they dictate an arbitrary exit point for the trader which sometimes may not be the best move. They, however, have to exit due to the internal control systems of the trader.

- Chart stop: as a result of price actions, chart indicators may sometimes create stops for the traders to avoid the losses. Technical indicator signals the traders when to exit. The chart shows the highs and lows and enables the traders when it is good to take the long or short position.

- Volatility stop: instead of using the price action it is better to use the volatility of prices to set the risk parameters. The idea in this is that in the high-volatility environments, the trader needs to be more adapted to avoid them being manipulated by the intra-market noise. For the low volatility markets, the opposite is applicable for the traders. Volatility in prices is a measure which deals with finding the variance of prices through standard deviation. However, an equity stop of around 2% should still be applicable to the trader's operations.

Conclusion

Forex trading is a business trend that has quickly gained popularity all over the world. With the digitalization of the Forex markets, it has become easier for anyone to trade in the markets even at the low equity investments. The problem still remains that people are venturing into the business without being well-prepared mentally or even psychologically. People need to have the basic information so that they can know what they are venturing in; without the information many people end up being on the loss and they are unable to recover from the loss and end up getting into debt. This book has explored the basics that a person venturing into Forex business needs to know. The information covered by this book is meant to help you understand the dynamics of the trade and how the trade happens. The definition of terms also helps traders to understand various terminologies during the actual business. With the discipline and vision, Forex markets can help you make a fortune even from a very minimal investment. Finding the right company to help you trade is also a vital part of the success in the industry.

Your Gift

I wanted to show my appreciation that you support my work so I've put together a free gift for you.

http://bonusfreebook.org/

Just visit the link above to download it now.

I know you will love this gift.

If you like this book, you can see and buy my other books on this link:

Thank you for attention!

With love,

Adam Clark

Legal & Disclaimer

The information contained in this book and its contents is not designed to replace or take the place of any form of medical or professional advice; and is not meant to replace the need for independent medical, financial, legal or other professional advice or services, as may be required. The content and information in this book have been provided for educational and entertainment purposes only.

The content and information contained in this book have been compiled from sources deemed reliable, and it is accurate to the best of the Author's knowledge, information and belief. However, the Author cannot guarantee its accuracy and validity and cannot be held liable for any errors and/or omissions. Further, changes are periodically made to this book as and when needed. Where appropriate and/or necessary, you must consult a professional (including but not limited to your doctor, attorney, financial advisor or such other professional advisor) before using any of the suggested remedies, techniques, or information in this book.

Upon using the contents and information contained in this book, you agree to hold harmless the Author from and against any damages, costs, and expenses, including any legal fees potentially resulting from the application of any of the information provided by this book. This disclaimer applies to any loss, damages or injury caused by the use and application, whether directly or indirectly, of any advice or information presented, whether for breach of contract, tort, negligence, personal injury, criminal intent, or under any other cause of action.

You agree to accept all risks of using the information presented in this book.

You agree that by continuing to read this book, where appropriate and/or necessary, you shall consult a professional (including but not limited to your doctor, attorney, or financial advisor or such other advisor as needed) before using any of the suggested remedies, techniques, or information in this book.